George Mason
Super Statesman

When George was nine, his father drowned in a boating accident while crossing the Potomac River.

George Mason was born December 11, 1725 on the Mason family plantation in Fairfax County, Virginia. His father was an English planter who owned land in Virginia and Maryland.

What year did George's father die?

1725 (Year George was born)

+ 9 (Age at the time of his father's death)

_____ (Year of his father's death)

©Carole Marsh/Gallopade International/800-536-2GET/www.virginiaexperience.com
This page is not reproducible.

George was tutored when he was a child. While he was still young, George went to study with his uncle, John Mercer, who was a lawyer. Uncle John had about 1,500 books. George read many of the books, especially the ones about the law.

Uncle John taught George lessons he would remember for the rest of his life.

"Pull" apart the words to make a sentence about George Mason.

Georgereadbooksaboutthenaturalrightsofmenandslavery.

John Mercer had one of the largest libraries in Virginia.

When George turned 21, he inherited his father's land. He had thousands of acres of farmland in Maryland and Virginia. George was a successful businessman. He farmed his lands and invested in the Ohio Company.

Scratch off every other letter starting with X to see what George supported.

The Ohio Company made money from buying and selling lands in the West.

XCGIMVJIULYLHINBBEGRTTRIFEVSC

Color the scales of justice.

On April 4, 1750, George married Ann Eilbeck. Ann was from a plantation in Charles County, Maryland. In 1755, George began building a new home. The house was finished in 1759.

George was 25 years old when he got married; Ann was 16.

Solve the code to discover the name of George's home.

In 1751, George was made the treasurer of the Ohio Company.

George and Ann had nine children. All of their children survived childhood. That was unusual in those days because of childhood diseases for which there were no cures.

George and his wife had five sons. How many daughters did they have?

(number of children)
(number of boys)
(number of girls)

George was elected to serve in the House of Burgesses in 1759, but he passed up opportunities to serve when it meant time away from his family.

In 1773, George's wife Ann died. That same year, George wrote his first major paper. It was called *Extracts from the Virginia*

Find the words in the Word Find below.

FREEDOM   RELIGION   PRE

In the fall of 1781, George provided supplies to colonial soldiers on their way to Yorktown for the final battle of the American Revolution.

When George Washington couldn't attend Virginia's Constitutional Convention in 1776, he asked George to go instead. George ended up writing the Virginia Constitution.

D	B	R	N
K	F	I	C
H	R	G	T
M	E	H	S
W	E	T	N
V	D	S	U
N	O	I	G
A	M	Y	S

Charters, With Some Remarks Upon Them. This paper helped the United States claim lands south of the Great Lakes.

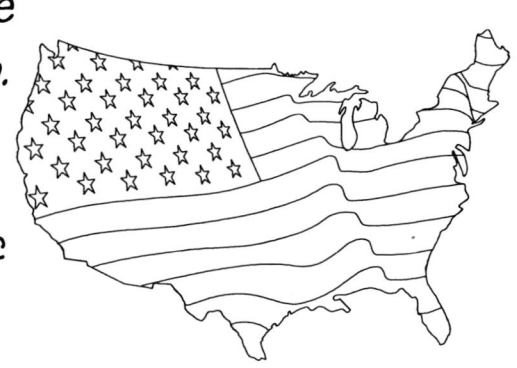

RIGHTS	VIRGINIA	GUNSTON	
A	S	K	N
I	S	B	I
N	E	U	F
I	R	H	O
G	P	U	R
R	B	J	U
I	L	E	R
V	D	K	W

George also wrote the Virginia Declaration of Rights, which states that all Virginians should have certain rights. These rights include freedom of religion and freedom of the press. The document became the basis for the Bill of Rights of the Constitution of the United States of America.

George was a member of Virginia's delegation to the Constitutional Convention in 1787. George made at least 136 speeches at the 1787 Constitutional Convention in Philadelphia. George believed that the House of Representatives should be based on a state's population.

Unscramble the letters to find out the name of a school in Fairfax, Virginia, named after George.

___ ___ ___ ___ ___ ___ ___
  E   O   R   G   G   E

___ ___ ___ ___ ___
  O   N   A   M   S

___ ___ ___ ___ ___ ___ ___ ___ ___
 E   T   Y   R   S   I   U   N   I   V

George also served on the committee that designed the great seal of the commonwealth of Virginia.

George refused to sign the U.S. Constitution because he felt it did not protect the rights of the people. His beliefs in personal freedom, however, inspired other delegates to work for the Bill of Rights.

 Much of what George wrote inspired Thomas Jefferson when writing the Declaration of Independence.

Number these events from George's life in the correct order.

_____ George leaves to study with his uncle.

_____ George marries Ann Eilbeck.

_____ George is born in Fairfax County, Virginia.

_____ George writes the Virginia Declaration of Rights.

George inspired James Madison to write the Bill of Rights for the United States Constitution.

Some people did not like George because he wouldn't sign the U.S. Constitution. But over the years, most of George's ideas became law. On October 7, 1792, George died at Gunston Hall.

Color the picture of George Mason.

George's Virginia Declaration of Rights has been called the first American bill of rights.

Glossary

civil liberties: basic rights guaranteed for all citizens by the law

commonwealth: a state, a country, or a group of states and countries

delegate: a person given power or authority to act for others; representative

House of Burgesses: the lower house of the colonial legislature in Virginia or Maryland

representative: a person appointed or elected to act or speak for others

seal: used to certify a signature or authenticate a document

Pop Quiz!

1. Where was George Mason born?
   - ○ Fairfax County, Virginia
   - ○ London, England
   - ○ Philadelphia, Pennsylvania

2. With who did George study law?
   - ○ His Father
   - ○ His Uncle
   - ○ His Mother

3. What was the name of George's home?
   - ○ Rumstown Hall
   - ○ Gunston Hole
   - ○ Gunston Hall

4. Which document became the basis for the Bill of Rights of the U.S. Constitution?
   - ○ Virginia Declaration of Rights
   - ○ Virginia Freedom of Rights
   - ○ Virginia and Philadelphia Freedom

5. What did George always support?
   - ○ Civil liberties
   - ○ Slavery
   - ○ U.S. Constitution